DID YOU KNOW?
APES AND MONKEYS ARE A LOT LIKE YOU
By: M. R. Kaye

M. R. Kaye

Copyright 2013 by M.R. Kaye
All Rights Reserved

No part of this book may be used or reproduced in any manner whatsoever without the written and signed permission of the author, except in the case of brief quotations

Due To The fact that most monkeys and apes live in protected areas we have done our best to source quality images for this book.

Unless otherwise mentioned all images are sourced according to CC0 Creative Commons and Fair Use. Attribution is given where required

Updated December 2018

TABLE OF CONTENTS

Publishers Notes
Aren't Apes & Monkeys the Same?
What Are Primates?
Ways That Apes and Monkeys Are Like Humans
How Apes and Monkeys Care For Their Babies
Types of Apes
Types of Monkeys
How to Protect Apes and Monkeys from Extinction
Endnotes

AREN'T APES & MONKEYS THE SAME?

One of the best parts about visiting a zoo is an opportunity to watch monkeys playing in trees or on swings and other equipment.

Apes can be fun to watch also, but you aren't likely to find monkeys in the ape house. At least, you shouldn't find them there.

Monkeys and apes, while both primates, are two separate types of animals. Monkeys are generally smaller and have tails while primates tend to be larger and tailless.

Several other characteristics set these two types of animals apart. Let's take a look:

Apes	Monkeys
• very intelligent • no tails • smooth, flat noses • can learn sign language	• not as intelligent • almost all have tails • snouts; not noses • can not learn sign language

To Sum it up. Apes are much more like humans than monkeys are.

Read More : http://bit.ly/MonkeyvApe

Hey, we're The Monkeys!

One of the biggest differences between apes and monkeys is where you can find them living in the wild.

Although apes can only be found in Asia and Africa, monkeys also live in Central and South America.

The two main categories of monkeys, Old World monkeys and New World monkeys have evolved differently over time.

Old World Monkeys

Old World monkeys, which come from the Cercopithecinae family, are **diurnal**, which means they run and play during the daytime like humans. Like all monkeys, they have tails, but they are unable to pick things up with their tails.

Generally larger than their New World cousins, Old World monkeys also have padded buttocks on which they can comfortably sit.

Vervet Monkey

Squirrel Monkey

New World Monkeys

New World monkeys are generally smaller than Old World monkeys. Most of them are active during the day like their cousins, but the owl monkey is nocturnal. It sleeps during the day and becomes active at night.

The Callitrichidae family of New World monkeys is smaller and contains Tamarins and Marmosets. Cebide monkeys, generally larger than those of the Callitrichidae family, include Owl and Spider monkeys.

Most of the monkeys in this family have prehensile tails, which means they can use their tails to pick up things the way humans use their hands.

Read More About Types of Monkeys
https://www.monkeyworlds.com

Going Ape

Apes, found in the wild only in Asia and Africa, generally grow much bigger and heavier than monkeys. They also have broad chests and no tail.

Unlike monkeys, apes rely more heavily on the senses of vision and hearing than on smell. Compared to other animals, apes have a higher brain to body-size ratio. Apes also have an upright body posture, and many types of apes prefer walking on two legs rather than four.

Lesser Apes

Lesser apes, known as **Gibbons**, are most likely to be confused with monkeys. Their small, slender bodies may look like those of monkeys, but looking closely, you'll notice that gibbons don't have tails.

Gibbons mate in pairs for life and tend to be less social than other apes.

Great Apes

Great apes have round faces and round, mostly hairless ears, and all great apes have the ability to walk upright on two legs.

Great apes communicate with a wide range of facial expressions and are capable of learning language, and they are expert problem solvers. If this sounds a lot like your family, that's because humans are great apes.

Other great apes include chimpanzees, orangutans, gorillas and bonobos. All great apes, like humans, live in complex social systems. In addition to being able to problem solve and learn language, great apes also use tools to help them accomplish tasks.

You And Me Are Primates Too

Monkeys and apes do have several things in common. After all, we're all primates. Except the spider monkey, all primates have five digits on each hand and foot.

In order to grasp and manipulate objects, primates have opposable thumbs. This means that the thumb can be rotated toward the fingers to establish a firm grip. All primates except for humans also have opposable big toes, which allow them to pick up and manipulate objects with their feet as well as their hands.

If you like to swim, climb trees or dance, you can be glad that you're a primate. Primates have more flexible shoulders and hips than most other mammals. This helps primates that live in the wild climb trees.

Did you know that your dog or cat has a much better sense of smell than you do? This is also because you happen to be a primate. Most primates, with the exception of lemurs, have relatively small noses. We also have smaller areas in the brain dedicated to processing the sense of smell.

Lemur

What primates lack in olfactory sense, however, we make up for with our enhanced vision. All great apes have color vision, and we are able to observe our surroundings and learn many things from what we see. Primates also tend to rely heavily on the sense of hearing.

Now You Know

No, monkeys and apes aren't the same animals. When you take your next trip to the zoo, remember that you should find monkeys in the rain forest exhibit but only apes will be in the ape house.

If Grandma or Mom affectionately refers to you as her "little monkey," that name isn't accurate. Next time, remind her that you are a great ape. Not only do you lack a tail, but you have a great brain. That brain and your nimble fingers, capable of using a pencil, scissors and other tools, give you a keen advantage in life.

Stand tall. Stand proud. You are a great ape. It's time to stop monkeying around.

WHAT ARE PRIMATES?

Primates are mammals covered with fur and they live in various environments. They can be found on most continents including Africa and South America.

Long ago, there was a higher population of primates but loss of natural habitat has reduced its numbers. The primate species includes Simians and Prosimians that have different physical characteristics and ways of living.

Most wild primates live in jungles or forested areas near lush vegetation such as shrubs, grass and trees. This variety of animal is usually a vegetarian, but scientists have occasionally observed certain primate species consuming meat such as insects.

There are several varieties of wild primate species living in remote areas away from humans.

Mountain Gorillas

Smaller primates often climb in trees to find foods such as nuts, berries and seeds. There are species of primates including gibbons that seldom touch the ground but travel from tree to tree with their long arms while holding on branches.

Mountain gorillas frequently weigh hundreds of pounds and are unable to climb trees. This species will search for food that falls from trees or grows on shrubs instead. Many primates have the ability to stand on their hind legs to reach for food in trees or walk for long amounts of time. Several species will alternate between walking on four or two limbs.

Primates range in size from tiny lemurs as small as a mouse to gorillas that weigh over 400 pounds. Many types of primate species will travel in groups with one large adult male, several smaller females and youngsters of various ages.

Males and females may have different color variations, tooth size and other traits to distinguish the genders. Primates tend to have large brains making it an intelligent animal that has the ability to learn new ways of gathering food such as using sticks to capture termites in a nest. Chimpanzees have learned to perform various tasks in circuses and zoos including following the directions given by trainers.

Intelligent Animals

Animal scientists believe many primates are intelligent because the animals have large eyes on the front of the head instead of on the sides. This allows the animals to focus better and see further away.

Many species of primates are able to make noises such as grunting, hooting or growling to communicate with each other. The animals might make a particular sound to alert other members of the group about a food source or a predator.

In zoos and animal sanctuaries, trainers have taught gorillas how to use sign language to communicate with each other and humans. A primate typically has very flexible hands and feet that are able to manipulate objects easily.

Flexible Hands

Instead of having long claws, primates have fingernails on five digits of each hand and foot. A primate's fingers and toes permit it to grip items while hunting and eating food. Many primate species have large bones and muscle mass, making the animals much stronger than humans of the same size and weight.

Primates rarely live alone because social groups are safer in the wild to avoid dangers from predators such as lions, hyenas or crocodiles. A primate family group typically works together to hunt for food sources, fight predators and raise infants. Each species has its own social pattern of cooperation that animal scientists often study for several years to understand completely.

Avoiding Dangerous Predators

While different species of primates including gorillas or chimpanzees avoid each other in the wild, there are species that cooperate as protection from dangerous predators. Many varieties of primates grow slowly and have longer lives than most animals do. Because this animal is a mammal, infants consume their mother's milk for several weeks or months. Usually, the infant's mother is its primary caregiver.

However, there are species that have males and other members of a group protecting and transporting the youngsters to new locations. Youngsters learn how to gather food, eat and escape danger over a long amount of time by watching other animals in the group.

Types of Foods Consumed

As the infant grows, it eventually learns to consume other foods such as fruit, insects or leaves. Several species have developed specialized diets including eating insect larvae, wild grass or tree gum.

Macaques and capuchin monkeys may eat lizards, fish and eggs instead. While hunting for food, primates must remain alert for dangers from animals including snakes, vultures and wild dogs. Within a primate social group, one or more animals might watch for danger as other members of the groups eats.

If danger occurs, the lookout animals make a sound alerting the other primates to run for shelter. Most species of primates live in rain forests on various continents. Hiding in the tops of trees is very common for many primates but several species live on the ground instead.

Protecting Primates from Extinction

The loss of natural habitat, disease and capture has reduced the number of many primate species. Hunters have captured large numbers of chimpanzees, gorillas and orangutans for circuses and zoos.

Many hunters kill primates to use the fur, body parts or meat. Unfortunately, health conditions such as measles can also transfer to several species of primates. Because the primates have no natural immunity, vaccination or medical treatment, many social groups die. Today, there are groups of people who protect primates by providing animal sanctuaries while fighting for laws that prevent killing the animals.

WAYS THAT APES AND MONKEYS ARE LIKE HUMANS

Apes and monkeys are like humans in several ways. From communication comparisons to DNA similarities, there is no denying that these primates are the closest relatives to humans. Let's dive in and take a close look at how we humans are the same as monkeys and apes. Or is that they are like us? No matter how one views it, the similarities are quite startling.

Cooking: Most people are unaware that monkeys and apes can cook. That's right. Give them a skillet and a pound of hamburger meat, and it's not uncommon for them to flatten the meat out, put it in the skillet, collect wood and light it with a match and fry a hamburger patty.

The primates don't usually know how to do this without instruction beforehand; however, showing them only one time is usually sufficient in them learning how to cook for their entire life. As the fire dies down, they will tend to go about collecting more wood, throwing it in to keep the fire going. They also stand far away from the fire to make sure they don't burn their selves.

DNA: The DNA found in humans, monkeys and apes is very similar. Some people argue that it is 99 percent the same; however, a more accurate estimate is somewhere between 85 to 95 percent.

Facial Expressions: Much of the communication that takes place among humans is through facial expressions. We also have certain words that we use when communicating a certain feeling. Monkeys and apes are the same. They tend to have certain hoots and pants that they use when communicating with other monkeys and apes. Their facial expressions used to act surprised, pleased, comforted, etc. are very much the same as humans' facial expressions.

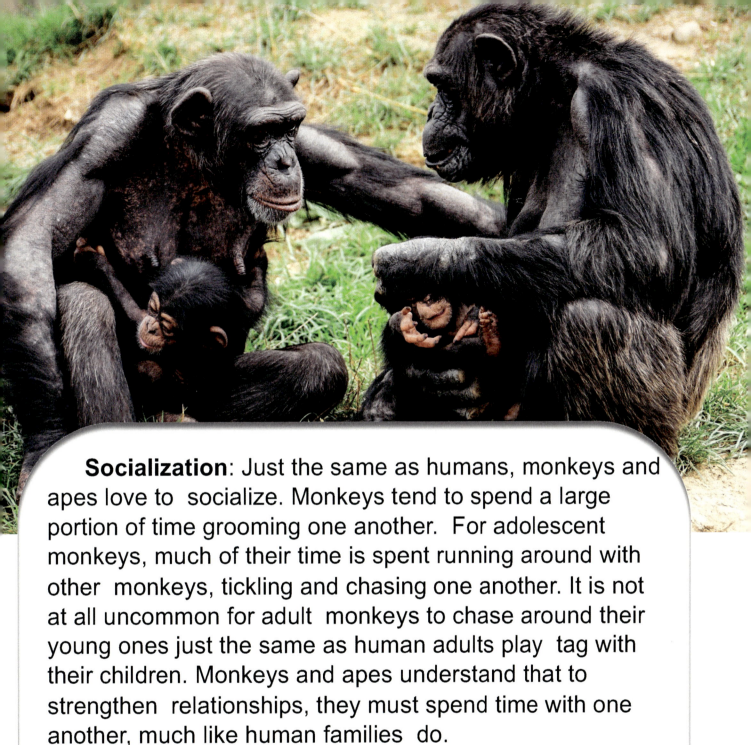

Socialization: Just the same as humans, monkeys and apes love to socialize. Monkeys tend to spend a large portion of time grooming one another. For adolescent monkeys, much of their time is spent running around with other monkeys, tickling and chasing one another. It is not at all uncommon for adult monkeys to chase around their young ones just the same as human adults play tag with their children. Monkeys and apes understand that to strengthen relationships, they must spend time with one another, much like human families do.

Walking Upright: Humans, monkeys and apes have the capability to walk upright. Although many primates move around on all fours, if they choose, they can walk on their feet. One of the reasons that monkeys and apes prefer to walk on all fours is that their hands tend to be stronger than their feet; this is because they often use their hands to crawl, climb, and swing and move in sideways or diagonal movements.

Eating:

Monkeys, apes and humans eat both plants and meats. While most monkeys tend to stick to a fruit and insect diet, it is not uncommon for them to hunt and eat mammals just the same as humans do with deer, squirrel, rabbit, etc.

Eyes: Some monkeys and apes have white around the iris in their eyes like humans. Monkeys, apes and humans can all see in color, which is beneficial for a wide range of reasons. It is mostly advantageous to monkeys and apes because it helps them to pick out ripe fruits. Humans and monkeys and apes are also the same in that they all have binocular vision, meaning both the eyes point in the same direction.

Using Money: there was a study conducted in Connecticut that concluded that monkeys and apes have the capacity to understand the concept of money. Just the same as us humans, the primates seek purchasing power, spending tokens on whatever it is that will get them the most for their 'dollar.' During the study, monkeys were given 12 tokens and told they could spend the money as they pleased on Jell-O, apples or grapes. When the price of one item increased, they would choose to spend less money on the cheaper items, which allowed them to get the most out of their money.

Gambling: Monkeys and apes like to gamble, and there is absolutely no denying that humans do too. In the same experiment referenced above, scientists discovered that when given the opportunity, the primates preferred to gamble.

The experiment conducted involved two lights. Looking at one light guaranteed the primates a certain amount of juice. Looking at the other light resulted in either a greater or smaller amount of juice. Even though much of the time looking at the second light resulted in less juice, the monkeys and apes preferred to gamble because of the thrill that it gave them.

Communication: When it comes to human communication, an important technique that is often used is sign language. As odd as it may seem, monkeys and apes have the capability to both learn and use sign language as well.

For those that are taught sign language, they will sometimes use it to communicate solely with humans; however, some of them communicate with one another through it as well. Monkeys and apes also have the capability to learn part of the English language. A gorilla named KoKo once learned more than 2,000 words found in the English language.

This is Kanzi, who learned to mimic human speech and shows advanced speaking skills.

HOW APES AND MONKEYS CARE FOR THEIR BABIES

Infant Care

Monkeys and apes are mammals that give birth to babies instead of laying eggs the way birds and reptiles do. Numerous species of apes and monkeys live in warmer climates in rain forests and jungle locations. Most wild monkeys and apes live on the continents of South America or Africa. However, a few species live in Asia or secluded islands. Research scientists frequently study primates to understand how the animals care for infants in native habitats. Of course, there are also many zoos or sanctuaries where a scientist can watch how apes and monkeys care for infants.

Cooperative Groups

Apes and monkeys usually live in cooperative groups in order to search for food and avoid predators. Mothers living in these groups often receive assistance from other members with caring for babies. This activity is unusual in many animal species but has several advantages in helping babies to survive. In addition, most monkeys and apes give birth to only one infant at a time making it easier to provide long-term care. Because only one infant is born at a time to a mother, it receives a lot of individualized attention.

Cleaning a Baby's Skin

Chimpanzee mothers often have babies late at night in a secluded area away from other members of a group.

After a baby is born, the mother will hold the infant and gently clean its hair and skin. Grooming is an important part of the bonding process for the mother and infant. This behavior also helps the infant and mother to recognize each other's particular scent.

Understanding the scent is important for chimpanzees because it assists in location when it is too dark to see. Because chimpanzees are a mammal, the mother nurses the infant for several months until it can eat regular food.

Protection from Danger

Mother chimpanzees allow other members of a group to help with the care of infants. This is an important part of survival when it is difficult to find food or escape predators in a dangerous jungle environment. Young infants will ride on a mother's back or stomach while clutching tightly when traveling to new locations.

Other chimpanzees in the group may carry infants when running from danger is necessary. Eventually, baby chimpanzees will begin consuming other foods such as fruit, seeds or leaves. A mother and other group members supervise the baby for several years.

How Babies Receive Food

At the same time, the baby is learning by observing its mother as she gathers food and communicates with members of the group.

A chimpanzee infant will remain near its mother receiving milk for nourishment for as long as six years. During this time, the baby will learn many skills such as how to find food including berries or termites.

Other adult members of a social group will bond with the infant by grooming its hair to remove insects or plant debris. Babies from different mothers will often play together as the adults watch carefully.

Babies Stay Close to Mothers

Monkeys are similar to apes in many ways, but one of the best ways to identify a monkey is by looking for a tail. Monkeys often have long prehensile tails that move due to having strong muscles.

Many monkeys use their tails to grasp on tree branches for extra support while collecting food or sleeping. There are over 250 species of monkeys that frequently live in trees instead of on the ground.

However, a few species of monkeys including baboons live primarily on the ground. Small monkey species may weigh just a few pounds while larger ones might weigh close to 100 pounds.

Mothers Hold Babies

Monkeys are intelligent mammals that give birth to live young that they nourish and take care of for several months or years.

Baboons are an old world monkey species that primarily lives in Africa and nearby regions.

There are five varieties of baboons that usually only have one infant at a time. A baboon mother will live in a group with several other baboons that cooperate to avoid predators while searching for food.

After a mother baboon has an infant, she allows it to ride on her stomach or back while it is still small and helpless.

Destroying Dangerous Parasites

This allows the mother to nurse the infant as she protects it from danger. A few baboon species share the care of infants within a group.

Occasionally, male baboons will kill infants to avoid competition as it grows. A baby baboon's mother will groom its fur frequently to prevent infestation from dangerous parasites. Mothers nurse an infant several times a day for approximately one year.

A male baboon will leave its cooperative birth group as it grows older to find mates in other groups. However, females remain with the same group their entire lives.

One Infant

Spider monkeys have extremely long arms, legs and tails that help them to travel through treetops. This new world monkey lives in social groups as protection from predators including humans.

Approximately every three years, an adult female will give birth to one infant.

Mothers carry infants on their stomach or back while it nurses. A baby spider monkey holds on its mother with its strong prehensile tail.

As the baby grows older, it will begin to look for different food sources. Male spider monkeys never assist with caring for infants within the cooperative groups.

TYPES OF APES

So, what's the difference between an ape and a monkey? Generally, an ape comes from Africa or Asia and doesn't have a tail. A monkey is usually smaller, has a tail and is native to both the Old and New Worlds. A human being can be classified as an ape, but for our purposes we're going to deal with those apes that still live in the wild. Here are some:

Gorilla

There are two types of gorillas. There's the western gorilla (gorilla gorilla) and the eastern gorilla (gorilla beringei).

The western gorilla is also called the lowland gorilla and lives in sub- Saharan Africa, including the Central African Republic, the Democratic Republic of Congo, Nigeria, the Republic of Congo and Cameroon. There's a subspecies of this gorilla called gorilla gorilla diehli, which lives near the border of Nigeria and Cameroon.

Western gorillas are big and powerful animals who have human looking faces though their brow ridges are far more prominent, their noses are flat and they have much larger nostrils.

They also have large and powerful jaws and teeth to help them chew their food, which is almost exclusively vegetarian. They're covered with dark hair and have black skin. As the males grow older, the hair on their back and rump starts to go attractively gray.

These males are known as silverbacks and are the leaders of their families. Males are bigger than females and can weigh as much as 600 pounds.

Gorilla Beringei, the eastern gorilla, lives in the cloudy, volcanic mountains found between the Democratic Republic of Congo, Uganda and Rwanda. They're smaller than the western gorilla.

These gorillas are striking because of their long, coarse hair. Their jaws are also larger and their arms are smaller than those of the western gorilla. Males also go gray as they age and are also called silverbacks.

Chimpanzee

The chimpanzee (pan troglodytes) is our closest relative and is said to share about 98 percent of our genes. However, it's that other two percent that make all the difference!

Chimpanzees are found in savannas and forests from Gambia to Uganda. There are three subspecies. One is P. troglodytes verus, P. troglodytes troglodytes and P. troglodytes schweinfurthi.

When chimpanzees stand up they can be between one to five and a half feet tall. The males are a bit larger than the females. Males can weigh up to 154 pounds while the females can weigh up to 110 pounds. Their arms are much longer than their legs and they have long hands, long fingers but short thumbs.

Longer thumbs would only interfere with them climbing the trees in their habitat. Their knuckles also help them to walk on all fours. Adult chimpanzees have a mostly hairless face with black or brown skin. Their fur is also black or brown and the fur of both sexes tends to thin out as they grow older.

Chimpanzee societies are complex and fascinating, with social hierarchies that can be quite fluid. Like humans, they take a long time to mature and seem to reach puberty when they're about seven years old though it can be many years before a female has her first baby. Female chimps often join other chimpanzee groups when they're mature.

A smaller and less hierarchical species of chimpanzee is the bonobo (pan paniscus). Along with the common chimpanzee, the bonobo is the closest relative to humans.

Orangutan

The Borneo orangutan (pongo pygmaeus) is found on the island of Borneo. It lives in the island's rainforests and unlike other apes is generally solitary. Borneo orangutans live mostly in the trees and rarely come down to the ground. Trees are where they find the fruit that is the mainstay of their diet.

Orangutans have startling orange hair, long arms and prehensile feet, which means they can hold on to branches with their feet as well as their hands. Both male and female orangutans have throat pouches though the males are larger.

The males are also considerably larger than the females. A male can weigh about 192 pounds while a female weighs only about 82 pounds. Males can also develop flanges or big cheek pads. Whether a male has flanges or not depends on his age and his position in orangutan social hierarchy. Borneo orangutans have smaller cousins who live in Sumatra.

Gibbon

There are several types of gibbons. They can belong to the nomascus genus, the hylobates genus, bunopithecus genus or symphalangus genus. All gibbons are monogamous.

The hoolick gibbon (bunopithecus hoolocki) is found in India, Bangladesh, Burma and the Southern part of China. It's found in mountainous, evergreen forests and is the second largest type of gibbon. It can weigh up to 18 pounds. It has long hair and like all gibbons, very long arms. Grown up males are all black but adult females are mostly dark brown and have some black around their chest, face and neck.

The siamang (Symphalangus syndactylus) is the largest type of gibbon. It can weigh over 26 pounds and be about three feet long. They're found in the tropical forests of Indonesia, specifically in Sumatra and the Malay Peninsula. Their coat is long and black and they have opposable thumbs, large canine teeth and a flat, almost hairless face. They're also notorious for having a huge throat sac that helps them amplify their calls. Siamang couples sing loud, rather unforgettable duets.

Siamangs are slow breeders and the female gives birth every two or three years or so to usually one baby. Siamangs are mature when they're around seven years old and have been known to live over 40 years in captivity. They probably don't live that long in the wild.

Other gibbons include the agile gibbon, black crested gibbon, red-cheeked gibbon, silvery gibbon, Kloss's gibbon and the pileated gibbon

TYPES OF MONKEYS

Many types of monkeys exist in the world. There is more than 260 different species of monkeys, and the monkeys come in various shapes, sizes and color combinations. There are three major groups of monkeys: New World primates, Old World primates and Apes. Old World primates are monkeys that come from areas in the world such as Africa and Asia.

New World primates come from Central and South America. Some people argue that apes are not really monkeys, but they have certain features that look similar to them. Apes do not have tails, however, and they are usually larger than the average monkeys.

Apes also have bigger chests than monkeys, and they can walk on both legs. Apes have larger brains than monkeys, and they live in Africa and Asia. The following contains more information about the different types of monkeys:

Types of New World Monkey

The Capuchin

The Capuchin Monkey is considered the smartest of all the New World monkeys. This monkey has a cream-colored body with dark arms and legs. A fully-grown Capuchin Monkey will only grow to be 2 pounds heavy and 22 inches tall. People can find these monkeys mostly in the lands of Argentina.

They eat a wide variety of foods during the day, and their meals consist of nuts, bugs, bird eggs, leaves and various fruits. At night, they hide from their predators and make sure they get plenty of rest for food hunting the next day.

The Squirrel Monkey

The Squirrel Monkey is a monkey that looks similar to a squirrel. It enjoys swamps and moist lands, and it usually travels in large groups. The Squirrel Monkeys eat a wide variety of foods such as twigs, insects and fruits. People can find their kind in places such as Venezuela and Bolivia. Some people have even spotted Squirrel Monkeys in parts of Florida. Their behavior is protective and excitable. The Squirrel Monkeys will make many sounds to let their onlookers know they are alive.

They don't look like Squirrels to me. What do you think?

The Golden Lion Tamarin

The Golden Lion Tamarin is a beautiful monkey that people can recognize by its thick golden coat. In some ways, this monkey resembles a small lion. A full-grown Golden Lion Tamarin will only grow to be approximately 16 inches. However, this monkey could have a tail that is more than 14 additional inches long.

The Golden Lion Tamarins will only live in the trees in a forest area. They usually stick together in the trees of Brazil, and they stay there throughout the night for rest. These monkeys eat only fruit, since they do not need a large quantity of food to survive.

The Howler Monkey

    The Howler Monkey is called such because of its tendency to become loud and boisterous. This Monkey is the loudest Monkey of all New World monkeys. A Howler Monkey will howl at the sun, the moon, the stars and everything in between. It also makes quite a bit of noise when it senses danger. Howler monkeys live in small groups and call on each other when they need help. They have large bodies and they move slowly. They enjoy snacking on fruits, nuts and leaves.

Types of Old World Monkeys

The Spectacled Langur

The Spectacled Langur is a peculiar looking monkey that has a scared, surprised or windblown expression. The hair on the Spectacled Langur's head also appears frizzy, which adds to the surprised look. It has excellent hearing and vision, which helps it to find food and stay out of danger's way.

The Spectacled Langur mostly eats vegetables and climbs trees. This monkey does not like to get into fights, but it is very vocal. The Langur loves to grunt, howl, bark and scream.

The Japanese Macaque

The Japanese Macaque is an interesting monkey. This type of monkey is also called the snow monkey, because of the gray coats on some of them. The Snow Monkey can also survive extremely cold temperatures, so it can play in the snow if it so desire.

Snow Monkeys mostly reside in Japan, but some have been discovered in parts of the U.S. such as Texas. Snow Monkeys like to eat leaves, twigs and fruits. They are very social monkeys, so they enjoy spending time with each other and playing in the snow together.

HOW TO PROTECT APES AND MONKEYS FROM EXTINCTION

Monkeys and apes are often grouped together when people are talking about them, as if they are one species. They are related, but they are very different in many respects. For example, apes tend to have broad chests and they are able to talk on their hind legs, like a human, whereas a monkey will be smaller and less powerful, and it will walk on all fours. At the same time, monkeys have tails, which they will use for swinging from one branch to another, but an ape will not have a tail. These are just a few of the many traits that set the two apart.

That being said, they are both being threatened with extinction if things are not done to protect them. In fact, some reports have stated that they could be extinct in as little as one generation. While this prediction might be sooner than it actually happens, and it would not apply to all types of monkey and apes, it does go a long way toward showing people just how real this threat is. Thankfully, there is still time to save them, and there are some important things that must be done to stop a very devastating extinction.

The Center For Great Apes is One Great Organization:
http://www.centerforgreatapes.org/

First of all, sickness is a threat. While it always has been in the wild, certain diseases are taking a higher toll now than they ever have before. One example is Ebola, which has taken the lives of many apes. It can spread through an entire group of them, decimating the population. Scientists need to work on finding a cure for Ebola so that they can administer it to the apes and save their lives. This would be research that could also help humans, so it is unclear why more has not already been done in this regard, but it should be done soon.

One of the larger reasons why apes and monkeys are nearing extinction, though, is because of human expansion. Did you know that there are more people alive now than the world has ever seen before?

This has forced cities and towns to expand, destroying the habitat for the apes and monkeys, who then die as they are forced to live somewhere that they were not meant to live. Humanity also brings with it disease and pollution, which can be very harmful.

Some effort should be made to expand into other places - seeing as how human population growth rates are not slowing down - that are not needed by primates.

Another reason is that these habitats are being destroyed by people who want to use the land. Sometimes they are looking to harvest rubber. Sometimes they just want to cut down the trees to use as lumber for building projects. Other times, they clear the land and burn the vegetation to make space for farming. All of these things leave the apes and monkeys in the area without anywhere to live. Steps need to be taken by local governments to make sure that the habitats are protected, that it is illegal for people to use the land in any fashion.

On top of that, you have to look at the impact of poaching. This is not as widespread as it once was, but it still does exist. Hunters will kill off many animals. Since they are operating outside of the law anyway, hunting when it is illegal, there is no limit to how many they can kill. Government law enforcement agencies must step up their work and really put an end to poaching once and for all. It is likely that more funds will be needed, both to monitor what is happening and to provide manpower to track down poachers.

Finally, some monkey and apes are used to test things that are then given to humans. These science experiments could test the potency of certain drugs or the impact of new cleaning products. Companies like to use these animals for the tests because they are so similar to humans. If the product has an adverse effect on the monkey or the ape, the company knows that the same thing is likely to happen to a human, so they can take steps to fix the problem.

To start with, it means that many animals that could be living in the wild are kept in captivity so that they can be used for testing. It also means that their very will to live can be sapped because they are not free and such destructive things are being done to them against their will. Finally, some of the monkeys and apes actually die during the testing process. They are then replaced with others who are captured, and this can take a huge toll on a local population if it is not stopped.

These are all things that have to change as soon as possible if the animals are going to be protected. People have to stop destroying their territory. They have to stop hunting them or killing them through tests and experiments. As much as possible, the human influence needs to be removed; save for positive influences, such as helping apes and monkeys to be protected from sickness and disease. If this is done and the primates are left in their communities, the population levels will rise once again and they will no longer be in such danger of extinction.

ENDNOTES

Thank you so much for spending time with us today.

If you enjoyed this animal book, would you please take a minute to leave a review on Amazon? Even just a couple of sentences would be great. When you leave a review, it helps others find my books for their children.

Thank You,

M. R Kaye

Find All My Books Here:
http://bit.ly/MRKayeAuthorPage

M.R. Kaye ©2013 -Did You Know? Series - Apes and Monkeys Are a Lot like You

Updated December 2018

Made in the USA
Monee, IL
27 November 2019